Half Hero

CW01663239

PAUL SHIPTON

Illustrated by Tim Archbold

OXFORD
UNIVERSITY PRESS

OXFORD
UNIVERSITY PRESS

Great Clarendon Street, Oxford OX2 6DP

Oxford University Press is a department of the University of Oxford.
It furthers the University's objective of excellence in research, scholarship,
and education by publishing worldwide in

Oxford New York
Auckland Cape Town Dar es Salaam Hong Kong Karachi
Kuala Lumpur Madrid Melbourne Mexico City Nairobi
New Delhi Shanghai Taipei Toronto

With offices in
Argentina Austria Brazil Chile Czech Republic France Greece
Guatemala Hungary Italy Japan Poland Portugal Singapore
South Korea Switzerland Thailand Turkey Ukraine Vietnam

British Library Cataloguing in Publication Data
Data available

ISBN: 978-0-19-911344-6

1 3 5 7 9 10 8 6 4 2

Available in packs
Stage 10 More Stories B Pack of 6:
ISBN: 978-0-19-911343-9
Stage 10 More Stories B Class Pack:
ISBN: 978-0-19-911344-6
Guided Reading Cards also available:
ISBN: 978-0-19-911352-1

Printed in China by Imago

1

No shoppers

Mr Dibley stared at the shop door and wished that someone would come in. It didn't work.

No one came to Dibley's any more. A Mega-Mart Superstore had opened across the street and everybody shopped there now.

'Let's stay open late,' said Alex, Mr Dibley's assistant.

'It won't help,' said Mr Dibley, sadly.

'I'll make the window display more exciting,' said Alex. She pointed at the three dummies in the window.

Just then, the door opened.

A shopper!

Alex jumped up. 'Can I help you?'

The man held up a map. 'How can I get to the Mega-Mart Superstore?' he asked.

'It's across the street,' said Alex. 'You can't miss it. It's big.'

Nobody else came in for the rest of the day.

'Tomorrow will be better,' said Alex.

'Let's hope so,' said Mr Dibley. 'If not, I'll have to close this shop down.'

He locked the door and set off for home. Alex rode off on her bike.

Inside the shop all was quiet, until ...

'Have they gone yet?' asked a voice from the window.

'Yes!'

'Is there anyone outside?'

'No!'

'Great! Let's go!'

2

What can we do?

The three plastic dummies in the shop window began to move.

'I thought they'd never go!' said Sale. She began to stretch and swing her arms.

'Careful!' Bargain warned. 'The last time you did that, your arms fell off. One of them hit me!'

'But I didn't hurt you,' said Sale. 'I was 'armless. Do you get it? Harmless? *Armless?*'

Sale and Bargain giggled. Bargain's wig slipped over his eye.

Little Half Price did not smile. 'Didn't you hear?' he said. 'Mr Dibley might shut the shop down. We'll lose our home!'

Sale and Bargain stopped laughing.

'We didn't think of that,' said Sale.

Half Price wasn't surprised – the big dummies didn't think of much.

'What can we do?' Bargain said.

Half Price scratched his plastic head. 'Let's try Alex's idea!' he said. 'We'll make the window display new and exciting!'

The big dummies loved this idea. They ran off to get new outfits.

'Half Price,' shouted Sale. 'Where are the sports things?'

'Over there, where it says: SPORTS,' said Half Price.

'Help, Half Price! These trousers won't go over my head,' shouted Bargain.

The dummies spent the night trying on outfits. The shop was in a terrible mess.

'Hurry!' said Half Price. 'Mr Dibley will be here soon. Remember the Golden Rule – *No one must know we can move by ourselves.*'

Bargain ran ... and crashed into Sale.

'Ow!' she said, and her arm dropped off. She grabbed it and bumped into Bargain. His head fell off.

He tried to pick it up, but he couldn't see what he was doing.

'Freeze!' shouted Half Price.
'Mr Dibley's here!'

3

Johnny Cashbucks

'Oh, dear,' said Mr Dibley when he saw the mess. 'I must have left a window open. The cat got in.'

It took him and Alex most of the morning to tidy up. The three dummies felt terrible, but they couldn't help or say sorry.

Alex went out for her lunch, and Mr Dibley sat and looked at the clock.

Just then, the door flew open and a big man walked in. 'My name is Johnny J. Cashbucks. I own the Mega-Mart Superstore across the road,' he boasted, 'and now I want to buy *your* shop, too.'

Mr Dibley loved his little shop, but he couldn't keep going without shoppers.

'I'll pay you lots of money!' Cashbucks said.

'Will you keep the shop the same?' Mr Dibley asked.

'I promise,' boomed Cashbucks, taking some papers from his pocket. 'Just put your name here.'

Mr Dibley looked at the papers.

At last he said, 'OK. I'll sell the shop.' He reached for his pen, but it wasn't in his pocket. 'I'll get a pen from the back room,' he said.

When Mr Dibley had gone, Cashbucks grinned. 'Yes, I *promise* ... to smash down this stupid shop. Then I can make the Superstore's car park even bigger!'

He didn't think anybody could hear him. But he was wrong ...

4

Breaking the Golden Rule

Bargain and Sale were scared. Half Price was moving and there was someone in the shop! Had the little dummy forgotten about the Golden Rule?

Half Price tiptoed to the back room door. Then he turned the key so that Mr Dibley couldn't get out.

Cashbucks heard the click of the key in the lock and turned around. He was surprised to see Half Price. He was even more surprised - MUCH more surprised - when the dummy spoke.

'Go away!' said Half Price. 'This is Mr Dibley's shop. He's not selling to YOU!'

Cashbucks froze in shock.

The big dummies were frozen, too.

'Come on, you two!' Half Price shouted to them. 'We've got to help Mr Dibley!'

'What about the Golden Rule?' Sale asked.

'If Cashbucks buys this shop, we'll lose our home!' said Half Price.

Bargain and Sale thought hard. (Thinking was *always* hard for them.) Then …

'Half Price is right!' shouted Sale. 'Clear off!' She shook her fist. It flew off and nearly hit Cashbucks.

'Yes!' Bargain shouted. 'Get out, NOW!' His head wobbled. It fell off and rolled across the floor.

'EEEK!' cried Johnny Cashbucks. He ran for the door.

'What's going on?' shouted Mr Dibley from the locked room.

Out in the shop, the big dummies were laughing.

'That showed him!' said Bargain, dusting off his head. 'He ran away when my head fell off!'

'No!' said Sale. 'It was when my hand almost hit him!'

'Quick! Let's get back in our places,' said Half Price.

The big dummies didn't listen.

'My head!' said Bargain.

'MY hand!' said Sale.

'It doesn't matter!' cried Half Price. 'Stop moving or someone else will see us!'

But it was too late. There was a crowd of people at the window, looking at the dummies.

5

New dummies

Alex was surprised to see a crowd outside the shop.

'What's going on?' she asked a man.

'The shop's got some amazing new dummies!' he said.

'They keep shouting and waving their arms at each other,' laughed a woman.

Alex pushed her way to the front.

The dummies were still.

'You missed them,' said a boy. 'Somebody must have turned them off.'

Alex wondered what everybody was talking about. But she had just had a good idea.

She shouted, 'Look at the fantastic clothes! And the low prices, too!'

'I *do* like that shirt on the dummy with the wobbly head,' said a man.

'Those prices *are* good,' said a woman.

'They're even lower, now!' cried Alex. 'We're having a sale!' She rushed inside ahead of the crowd and found Mr Dibley locked in the back room.

'What's going on?' he cried.

'No time to explain!' said Alex. 'We've got lots of shoppers!'

Mr Dibley smiled. 'Let's start selling!' he said.

After that, Mr Dibley put Alex in charge of picking trendy new clothes. Soon the shop was always busy.

One or two shoppers asked about the amazing moving dummies. Mr Dibley always said politely that they must have made a mistake. Dibley's dummies could not move.

In the end, people stopped asking, but they didn't stop coming to the shop.

Johnny Cashbucks never tried to buy the shop again. He wouldn't go near it. He went on holiday, saying he needed a very long rest.

Half Price, Bargain and Sale were careful not to break the Golden Rule again.

But sometimes Alex would find a few outfits in the wrong places.

Then she would gaze at the dummies and think about the day when people had said they moved.

The next time Alex was changing the window display, she looked right in Half Price's plastic eyes.

In the evening light, it seemed to her as if the little dummy gave a big smile.

About the author

When I was growing up in Manchester, I always wanted to be an astronaut, a footballer, or (if those didn't work out for any reason) perhaps a rock star. So it came as something of a surprise when I became first a teacher and then an editor of educational books.

When I was young, I never liked going shopping. (I still don't, unless it's for books or CDs!) I used to look at the shop dummies and wonder if they were as bored as I was!